AUTHENTIC AND TR. POLISH RECII

CW01065272

Inspired by Babcia's big black book of recipes.

By

ANNA NOVAK

INTRODUCTION

I have my Grandmother (Babcia) to thank for igniting my passion for Polish cuisine at a very young age. I remember all the fantastic smells, the rolling out of the pastry for pierogi and getting covered flour. My favorite part, eating and enjoying all this love spread out over the table.

My aim in this book is to help you relive those memories and create new memories with cooking Traditional Polish food, that you can recreate at home.

The book consists of 15 easy to follow recipes that are Authentic and Traditional. I have selected (with the help of Babcia) 5 soup, 5 main and 5 desert dishes.

Buy this book today and start enjoying the simplicity of Polish cooking.

Thank You and happy cooking!

TABLE OF CONTENTS

Traditional Polish Cabbage and Sauerkraut Soup "Kapusniak"

Prep Time: 25 minutes
Cook Time: 130 minutes
Total Time: 155 minutes
Yield: 10-12 servings

INGREDIENTS:

- 4 slices chopped bacon
- 1 large chopped onion
- 2 celery ribs cut into 1/4-inch slices
- 4 Carrots peeled and cut
- 2 large potatoes, peeled and cut into dices
- 2 cloves garlic, minced
- 1 small head of shredded cabbage
- 2 pounds' fresh pork spareribs, cut into 2-rib pieces
- 1 ham on the bone or hock
- 1-pound sauerkraut, drained (save juice and put to side)
- 8 ounces' tomato sauce
- 4 quarts' beef stock
- 1 teaspoon sweet paprika
- 1 bay leaf
- 2 tablespoons sugar
- Chopped parsley for garnish
- Sour cream

PREPARATION:

1. In a stock pot, sear pork ribs on both sides over medium-high heat. This takes no longer than a few minutes and once seared, remove the ribs from the pot and put to side.

2. Add bacon to pot and fry until tender. Add onions, celery, carrots, potatoes and garlic to the pot and cook until onion is silky smooth. Add fresh cabbage and cook until it loses its firmness and is cooked. Return spareribs to the pot and add ham bone or hock, sauerkraut, tomato sauce, beef stock, paprika, bay leaf and sugar. Mix well. Bring to a boil. Reduce heat to medium low and cook about 2 hours or until meat falls away from the bones.

3. Remove ribs and ham bone or hock from the soup, let it cool slightly then remove all bones and cartilage from meat. Chop meat into bite-size pieces, if necessary, and return to the pot. If you prefer a sourer soup, add the reserved sauerkraut juice.

4. Allow the soup to cool first, then refrigerate. The next day, skim off fat and reheat. (The reason its best to eat the soup the second day is because all the beautiful flavors are settled and sealed in) Serve with a dollop of sour cream and sprinkle of chopped parsley.

PICKLED CUCUMBER SOUP "ZUPA OGORKOWA"

Prep Time: 15 minutes
Cook Time: 30 minutes
Total Time: 45 minutes
Yield: 8-10 servings

INGREDIENTS:

- 1 large onion, finely chopped
- 3 cloves garlic, finely chopped
- 4 medium carrots, peeled and diced
- 3 celery stalks, diced
- 2 large bay leaves
- 5 allspice berries
- 2 x 32 fl oz chicken broth
- 2 chicken breast halves
- 3 medium potatoes, peeled and diced
- 1 jar of Polish pickles in brine (1 lb, 15 oz.), coarsely grated. Drain pickles, reserve pickle juice
- 1 tablespoon butter
- 1 container (32 oz.) of sour cream
- 2 tablespoons flour
- 4 tablespoons fresh dill
- Salt and pepper to taste

PREPARATION:

1. In a large pot, sauté the onion in olive oil until it becomes translucent. Add the garlic and continue cooking, stirring, just until the garlic is ready. Add carrots, celery, bay leaves and allspice and sauté for 5 more minutes

2. Add broth and chicken breasts, bring to a simmer and cook for 15 minutes

3. As the carrots and celery start to get soft, add the potatoes and salt and pepper to taste.

4. Separately, sauté the shredded pickles in the butter for about 5 minutes. Once sautéed add pickles and pickle juice to the soup.

5. When cooked, remove the chicken from the soup and cut into small pieces and return back to the soup.

6. In a small bowl, beat sour cream and flour thoroughly until smooth.

7. Slowly add sour cream mixture to soup, while stirring so it will remain smooth. This takes only a few minutes and you will know when done as the soup will thicken more. Add dill as garnish when serving.

Beetroot Soup "Barszcz czerwony"

Prep Time: 45 minutes
Cook Time: 120 minutes
Total Time: 165 minutes
Yield: 8-10 servings

Ingredients:

- 1 1/2 pounds' pork spare ribs
- 1 large onion, chopped and diced
- 1 bay leaf
- 3 peppercorns
- 2 tablespoons white vinegar
- 5 medium beets
- 2 cups sour cream
- 2 cups milk
- 3 tablespoons flour
- Salt and pepper

Preparation:

1. In a large pot add the spare ribs, onion, bay leaf, peppercorns, vinegar and cover with water. Bring to a simmer and cook until the meat is tender, about 1 to 1 1/2 hours.

2. In another pot, add scrubbed beets, cover with water and bring to a boil. Simmer the beets for 45 mins or until the beets are

tender. Drain and rinse the beets under cold water until cool. Peel and grate the beets. (I would suggest using gloves when handling and preparing the beets as they will stain your hands!)

3. When the meat is tender, Remove the bones and strip off the meat in bite size pieces. Return the meat to the broth and stir in the grated beets. At this time add the salt and pepper.

4. In a large bowl stir together the sour cream, milk and flour. Add two cups of the hot stock to the sour cream mixture and stir to combine. To make it extra smooth pour the mixture through a strainer into the soup.

5. Heat the soup over medium heat at a gentle simmer, do not allow it to boil! Boiling will cause the sour cream to curdle.

6. Serve immediately with boiled potatoes or rye bread to follow with traditions.

Polish Rye meal soup "Zurek"

Prep Time: 20 minutes
Cook Time: 30 minutes
Total Time: 50 minutes
Yield: 4 servings

Ingredients:

- 3 cloves of garlic
- 3 bay leaves
- 2 cups of warm water
- 2 white sausages, chopped
- 1/2 bunch parsley
- 1 medium-size onion
- 3 potatoes
- 3 tbs. thick sour cream
- 1 tbs. of marjoram
- salt & pepper to taste
- 4 hard-boiled eggs

Preparation:

To make the rye meal sour base (żur or kwas):

1. Pour the rye flour into clay pot and add the pressed garlic.

2. Pour warm water into mixture. Mix until consistent and slightly thicker.

3. Leave for 4 to 5 days in a warm place, windowsill is perfect. You will know when the sour base is ready because of the distinctive sour smell.

To MAKE THE SOUP:
1. Pour rye meal sour base into a large pot, add a cup of water, (taste to make sure it's not too sour, if too sour add a little water) and bring to a boil.

2. When boiling, add the parsley, bay leaves, marjoram, chopped white sausage and salt and pepper for seasoning.

3. In a separate pot boil the potatoes.

4. Cook until soup gives off a strong aroma. Around 45min-1hour.

5. Turn off heat, add sour cream, eggs, and boiled potatoes. Stir and serve.

Forrest Mushroom Soup "Zupa Grzybowa z Borowikow z Lazankami"

Prep Time: 30 minutes
Cook Time: 30 minutes
Total Time: 60 minutes
Yield: 6 servings

Ingredients:

- ½ ounce dried mushrooms (oyster, porcini)
- 2 large potatoes
- 1 large carrot
- 1 celery stalk
- 1 bay leaf
- 4 cups water
- 1 teaspoon salt, divided
- 2 tablespoons butter
- 8 ounces' fresh mushrooms, sliced
- 1 large onion, finely diced
- 2 tablespoons parsley
- 1 cup sour cream
- 1 tablespoon lemon juice

Preparation:

1. Put the dried mushrooms in a bowl and pour 1 cup hot water over them. Allow to sit 2-4 hours or until rehydrated.

Cut the carrot into small bite-sized pieces. Peel and dice the potato. Mince the celery. Add to large pot with 4 cups water, add ½ teaspoon salt, and bay leaf. Bring to fast boil and then reduce heat and simmer for 15 mins, or until the potato and carrots are tender. Don't worry if the potatoes break up, its adds an extra layer of texture.

Heat butter in a large skillet over medium-high heat and sauté onion and mushrooms with remaining ½ teaspoon salt. Drain the soaked mushrooms, slice and keep juice to the side. Add sliced mushrooms to pan along with the soaking juice (use a strainer to add the juice as this prevents dirt getting into the soup.)

Simmer the mushrooms and onions until liquid has been absorbed.

Now add to the vegetables and broth. Add parsley and simmer 10 minutes.

Stir in sour cream and lemon juice at the end.

POTATO AND CHEESE DUMPLINGS "RUSKIE PIEROGI"

Prep Time: 45 minutes
Cook Time: 15 minutes
Total Time: 60 minutes
Yield: 30 Pierogis

INGREDIENTS:

TO MAKE THE DOUGH:

- 2 to 2 1/2 cups plain flour
- 1 large egg
- 1 teaspoon salt
- 1 cup warm water

POTATO-CHEESE FILLING:

- 2 pounds' potatoes,
- 2 tablespoons minced onion
- 1 tablespoon butter
- 8 ounces' ricotta
- Salt and pepper

PREPARATION:

1. Peel potatoes and fork blend (do not mash) and mix with sautéed onion and ricotta cheese. Season with salt and pepper and set aside.

2. Place 2 cups flour in a large bowl or work surface and make a well in the center. Break the egg into it, add the salt and a little lukewarm water at a time. Bring the dough together, kneading well while adding more flour or water if necessary. Put dough into a bowl, cover with cloth or plate and allow to rest 20 minutes.

3. On a floured work surface, roll the dough out thinly and cut with a 2-inch round or glass. Spoon a portion of the filling into the middle of each circle. Fold dough in half, cover the filling and pinch edges together. Repeat process until all the filling or dough is all used.

4. Sprinkle a baking tray with flour and place the filled pierogi on it and cover with tea towel. Bring a large saucepan of salted water to boil. Drop in the pierogi (around 8 per time.) When the pierogi rise to the surface, simmer for 2 more minutes.

5. Remove pierogis and allow to drain. Traditionally "Ruskie Pierogies" are served with fried off bacon cubes and sautéed onions. This only takes a few minutes so I usually do this while the pierogis are draining. Sprinkle the bacon and onion over pierogis and serve.

Breaded Pork Cutlet "Kotlety schabowe"

Prep Time: 15 minutes
Cook Time: 15 minutes
Total Time: 30 minutes
Yield: 4 Cutlets:

INGREDIENTS:

- 1-pound pork tenderloin
- Salt and pepper
- 1 cup all-purpose flour
- 1 large egg beaten
- 1 teaspoon water
- Bread crumbs
- Canola oil

PREPARATION:

1. Trim fat off tenderloin, and cut into 4 equal pieces. Pound pork between two pieces of plastic wrap till ¼ inch thick (You may like the pork to be thicker so you can skip the pounding,) Season both sides with salt and pepper.

2. In 3 separate bowls, flour beaten egg and bread crumbs. In this order, cover the pork (one at a time) in flour (this is to dry it) place pork into beaten egg (this is to moisten pork for the crumbs to

stick) then cover pork in bread crumbs. Set aside for 10 mins.

3. Heat canola oil to a depth of 1 inch in a large skillet. Add two pork cutlets at a time. Fry 5 minutes per side or until golden. (The side dishes that are typically served with the pork cutlet are boiled potatoes and shredded, cooked beetroot.)

BAKED TROUT WITH GARLIC BUTTER "PSTRĄG Z MASŁEM CZOSNKOWYM"

Prep Time: 20 minutes
Cook Time: 20 minutes
Total Time: 40 minutes
Yield: 4 servings

INGREDIENTS:

- 2 crushed garlic cloves
- 2 ounces (1/2 stick) butter
- 4 medium whole trout (scaled and cleaned) with heads and tails on
- 1 Lemon
- Salt and pepper
- Parsley

PREPARATION:

1. Heat oven to 400 degrees. Coat a large baking pan with cooking spray. Make the garlic butter by mixing garlic and butter (make sure butter is warm and soft) in a small bowl, and set aside.

2. Prepare trout by rinsing in water and drying with paper towel. Use lemon juice inside and outside of trout, then with salt and pepper.

Put fish on baking pan and cover with foil. Bake 10 minutes.
Remove foil and bake an additional 10 minutes or until fish flakes.

Place trout on plates. Drizzle garlic butter over fish. Garnish with
lemon slices and a sprinkle of parsley.

Stuffed Cabbage with tomato sauce
"Gołąbki"

Prep Time: 30 minutes
Cook Time: 60 minutes
Total Time: 90 minutes

Ingredients:

- 1 whole cabbage, around 4 pounds
- 1 large onion
- 2 tablespoons butter
- 1-pound ground beef
- 1/2-pound ground pork
- 1 1/2 cups cooked plain white rice
- 1 teaspoon finely chopped garlic
- 1 teaspoon salt
- 1/4 teaspoon black pepper
- 1 cup beef stock
- 1 tablespoon tomato paste

Preparation:

1. Heat oven to 350 degrees.

2. Remove core from cabbage and place in large pot filled with boiling, salted water. Cook until leaves are soft and tender, around 3 mins.

3. When leaves are cool use knife to cut away the thick center stem from each leaf.

4. Chop the remaining cabbage and place it in the bottom of a casserole dish.

5. Sauté onion in butter in a large frying pan until tender, and put aside to cool.

6. Mix cooled onions with beef, pork, rice, garlic, salt and black pepper until well combined.

7. Place about 1/2 cup of meat on each cabbage leaf. Roll away from you to encase the meat. You then need to form tight 'envelopes' repeat process until all done.

8. Place the cabbage rolls on top of the chopped cabbage in the casserole dish, Season with salt and pepper. Pour beef stock over rolls with tomato paste, cover and place in oven. Bake till cabbage is tender, around 1 hour.

9. Serve with left over tomato sauce from casserole dish and drizzle over each cabbage roll before serving.

Hunters Stew "Bigos".

Prep Time: 30 minutes
Cook Time: 90 minutes
Total Time: 120 minutes
Yield: 6-8 servings

Ingredients:

- 1/2 medium cabbage;
- 4 cups of sauerkraut;
- 1 can tomato paste;
- 1/2-pound bacon sliced;
- 1-pound pork diced
- 1-pound Kielbasa sausage
- ¼ pound chopped mushrooms
- 1 large onion diced;
- 2 cloves garlic minced;
- 1 bay leaf;
- Salt and pepper

Preparation:

1. Cut cabbage in thin slices and boil until tender in a pot, around 5 minutes.

2. Boil the sauerkraut in another large pot with 2 cups of water. Strain and keep juice.

3. Sauté diced pork in a pan with some cooking oil then set aside.

4. Sauté the bacon and sausage with the onion and garlic.

5. In a large pot, combine the cooked cabbage, sauerkraut, juice, tomato paste, sautéed meats, onion, garlic, mushrooms, salt and pepper. Let simmer for 1 hour then serve.

APPLE PIE "JABŁECZNIK"

Prep Time: 20 minutes
Cook Time: 40 minutes
Total Time: 60 minutes
Yield: 12 servings

INGREDIENTS:

DOUGH:

- 3 cups plain flour
- 6 tablespoons powdered sugar
- 1 ½ tablespoons baking powder
- ½ cup butter,
- ¼ cup natural yogurt
- 3 egg yolks
- 3-4 Tablespoons cold water

FILLING:

- 10 large apples
- 2 Tablespoons warm water
- 1 Tablespoons lemon juice
- 2 Tablespoons cinnamon
- 2 Tablespoons plain flour

PREPARATION:

MAKE THE DOUGH

. Preheat the oven to 350°F.

. Mix flour, powdered sugar and baking powder in a large bowl. Cut in butter until the mixture resembles coarse crumbs.

. Mix in yogurt and egg yolks until combined. If crust is too crumbly to hold together, add 1 tablespoon of cold water.

. Divide the crust into two pieces, roughly ⅔ and ⅓ of the dough. Wrap the smaller section in plastic wrap and refrigerate for 30 minutes. Roll the larger section out into a 9" circle, and place into the bottom of a greased and floured 9" spring form pan.

. Prick the bottom crust with a fork and bake for 15 minutes.

MAKE THE FILLING

. While the crust is baking, mix the apples, water, lemon juice and cinnamon in a large pot. Heat over medium to high until the apples soften, about 3-5 mins. Add flour and simmer, uncovered, stirring until thicker, around 5 mins. Remove from heat and let cool slightly.

Assemble the Cake for Baking

1. When the crust is golden, remove it from the oven onto a cooling rack. Spread the filling over the warm crust. Take the last ⅓ of crust out of the refrigerator and grate it over the apple filling using a cheese grater.

2. Return the pie to the oven and bake for 30-45 minutes, or until the top is golden.

3. Remove the pie from the oven and let stand for 15 minutes before removing the spring-form support.

Polish Cheese cake "Sernik"

Prep Time: 20 minutes
Cook Time: 60 minutes
Total Time: 80 minutes
Yield: 8-12 slices

Ingredients:

Crust:

- 1 1/4 cups plain Flour
- 1/4 tablespoon Salt
- 3/4 tablespoon Baking Soda
- 1/4 cup Butter
- 1 whole Egg
- 3 Tablespoon Sour Cream
- 1/3 cup Confectioners' Sugar

Filling:

- 6 whole Eggs (1 separated)
- 2 cups Confectioners' Sugar
- 1 1/2 tablespoon Vanilla Extract
- 1 lb. Farmers or Ricotta Cheese
- 2/3 cup Butter, melted
- 1 1/2 cups plain Mashed Potatoes
- 2 tablespoons Baking Powder
- 1/2 tablespoon Nutmeg
- 1/2 tsp. Salt
- 1/4 cup Orange or Lemon Peel, grated

PREPARATION:

MAKE THE CRUST

1. Sift together the flour, salt, and baking soda in a large mixing bowl, then cut in the butter with a fork. Place the dough on a lightly floured surface and knead until well mixed and smooth.

2. In a separate mixing bowl, beat together the egg and sour cream. Stir the mixture into the flour. Add the confectioner's sugar and blend again.

3. On a floured surface, roll out the dough into the shape of a rectangle. Line a 9-inch by 13-inch pan with the dough. Make sure the dough covers half way up the sides of the tray.

Make the Filling

1. Separate 1 egg and reserve the egg white, beat the remaining yolk and five whole eggs with mixer in a small mixing bowl, gradually adding the confectioners' sugar as you go. Beat for 5 minutes at high speed. Add the vanilla and continue to beat at a high speed until the mixture is soft, around 2 minutes.

2. In a separate mixing bowl, press the cheese through a sieve and blend with the melted butter. Add the potatoes, baking powder, nutmeg, and salt.

3. Thoroughly blend all the ingredients and fold them into the egg mixture, then add the filling into the crust in the baking pan.

4. Wrap the excess dough over the top of the filling and pinch to close the gap as you go. Brush the top with the remaining egg white, and bake in a pre-heated 350-F degree oven for 45 to 55 minutes, or until set.

5. Let cool down before cutting. Refrigerate to store, but serve at room temperature.

ANGEL WINGS "CHRUSCIKI"

Prep Time: 15 minutes
Cook Time: 10 minutes
Total Time: 25 minutes
Yield: 6 dozen

INGREDIENTS:

- 5 egg yolks
- 1 large whole egg
- 1/2 teaspoon salt
- 1/4 cup confectioners' sugar
- 1/4 cup heavy cream
- 1 teaspoon vanilla
- 1 tablespoon rum or brandy
- 2 cups plain flour
- Vegetable oil

PREPARATION:

1. Combine egg yolks, whole egg and salt in mixing bowl. Beat at high speed until thick and lemon colored, about 5 minutes. Beat in sugar, cream, vanilla and rum. Add flour and beat until bubbles form, about 5 minutes.

2. Turn dough out onto a floured board, divide in half, cover with plastic wrap and allow to rest for half an hour.

Using half the dough at a time, roll out to 1/8-inch thickness. Cut into 2-inch-wide strips. Cut these strips on the diagonal at 4-inch intervals.

Heat 2 inches of oil in a large, deep skillet to 350 degrees. Make a slit in the center of each strip of dough. Then pull one end through the slit to form a bow.

Fry no more than 6 at a time for 1 minute per side or until golden. Drain on paper towels. Dust with confectioners' sugar. They are best to be consumed on the same day of cooking as they tend not to keep too long.

POLISH DOUGHNUTS "PĄCZKI"

Prep Time: 10 minutes
Cook Time: 30 minutes
Total Time: 40 minutes
Yield: 2 dozen

INGREDIENTS:

- 1 1/2 cups milk
- 2 packages active dry yeast
- 1/2 cup sugar
- 4 ounces (1 stick) butter
- 1 large egg
- 3 large egg yolks
- 1 tablespoon brandy or rum
- 1 teaspoon salt
- 4 1/2 to 5 cups plain flour
- 1-gallon oil for deep frying
- Granulated sugar

PREPARATION:

1. Add yeast to milk, stir and set aside. In a large mixer beat cream, sugar and butter until fluffy. Beat in egg, egg yolks, brandy or rum, and salt until beaten thoroughly

2. In the same mixer add 4 1/2 cups flour (add in gradually.) Add the yeast and milk mixture and beat for 5 more minutes until smooth. The dough should be soft and loose. If too soft add more flour.

3. Place dough in a greased bowl. Cover and let rise until doubled in size. Up to 2 hours.

4. Turn dough out onto floured surface. Roll out to 1/2-inch thickness. Cut rounds 3-inch diameter. Cover and let rounds rise until doubled in bulk, around 30 minutes.

5. Heat oil to 350 degrees in large skillet. Place bulked round dough into hot oil one at a time and fry 2 to 3 minutes or golden brown. Flip over and fry another 1 to 2 minutes or until golden brown. Be sure not to let the oil get too hot as the outside will cook before the center is done.

6. Drain pączki on paper towels and roll in granulated sugar while still warm. You also have freedom to add almost any filling you desire. If you would like to add a filling, say plum jelly, simply make a hole in the side and pump in the filling.

POLISH APPLE PANCAKES "RACUSZKI Z JABŁKAMI"

Prep Time: 30 minutes
Cook Time: 10 minutes
Total Time: 40 minutes
Yield: 4-6 servings

INGREDIENTS:

- 3 large apples
- 2 large eggs
- 2 cups plain flour
- 2 cups lukewarm milk
- 3 tablespoons melted butter
- 1 tablespoon vanilla extract
- 2 tablespoons dry instant yeast
- 1 tablespoon sugar
- 1/4 tablespoon salt
- 3/4 cup oil for frying
- Icing sugar for serving

PREPARATION:

1. Mix all the dry ingredients in large mixing bowl. Do not add the icing sugar.

2. Add eggs, vanilla and milk in to the flour mixture and whisk until all ingredients are blended. Be sure the mixture is creamy and thick, if not thick add more flour. Set aside and allow to rest for 1 hour.

3. Peal the apples, remove core and cut into small pieces.

4. Once dough has rested add apples and mix.

5. Heat oil in pan to medium, pour enough batter to make the pancakes the size you desire. Fry for about 2 minutes, each side, or until golden brown.

6. Sprinkle with icing sugar and serve.

CAN I ASK A FAVOR?

If you enjoyed this book, found it useful or otherwise then I'd really appreciate it if you would post a short review on Amazon. I do read all the reviews personally so that I can continually write what people are wanting.

Thanks for your support!

Printed in Great Britain
by Amazon

54570796R00030